Exposure at Default of Unsecured Credit Cards

Min Qi*

Office of the Comptroller of the Currency

July 2009

OCC Economics Working Paper 2009-2

Abstract

Retail exposure at default (EAD) is one of the weakest areas of risk measurement and modeling in industry practices and in academic literature. The U.S. Basel II Final Rule is not specific about the approach to EAD. In this study, we use borrower and account information from a large national sample of unsecured credit card defaults to capture borrower and lender behavior as borrowers approach default and to measure and model loan equivalent (LEQ), a common approach to EAD estimation. Dynamic snapshots of account credit limits and balances indicate that borrowers are more active than lenders in the "race to default." We find that a little over a dozen borrower, account, and macro factors are significant drivers of EAD. Models incorporating these risk drivers show improved predictive accuracy. Our study offers a useful benchmark to banks' EAD models and fills the void in the literature on retail EAD.

Key Words: Exposure at Default (EAD), Loan Equivalent (LEQ), Credit Card, Basel II
JEL Codes: G21, G28

* Credit Risk Analysis Division, Office of the Comptroller of the Currency, 250 E St. SW, Washington, DC 20219; voice: 202-874-4061; fax: 202-874-5394; e-mail: min.qi@occ.treas.gov. I am grateful to Regina Villasmil for her excellent research assistance and to Dennis Glennon and Gary Whalen and Risk Analysis Division Seminar participants for helpful comments and suggestions that have improved this work. The views expressed in this paper are those of the author and do not necessarily reflect the views of the Office of the Comptroller of the Currency or the U.S. Department of the Treasury.

1. Introduction

Credit cards, home equity lines of credit, and revolving lines of credit are examples of revolving retail exposures, whereas mortgages, auto loans, and home equity loans are examples of term loans. There are many differences between revolving exposures and term loans—for example, revolving exposures are open-ended, while the term loans are close-ended; borrowers pay interest only on funds drawn from the revolving credit; and a qualifying revolving exposure (QRE) is unsecured and unconditionally cancelable by the lender to the fullest extent permitted by federal law. In terms of repayment, the interest and principal payment of term loans are usually equal monthly installments over the life of the loan, whereas revolving credits allow the consumer to repay any amount at any time as long as the preestablished minimum monthly payment is met.

Revolving retail credit products offer convenience and financial flexibility that term loans lack. They can provide borrowers access to funds when deterioration in credit quality prevents them from borrowing through other credit channels. Agarwal, Ambrose, and Liu (2006) studied home equity line utilization at and after origination and found that borrowers with greater expectations of a decline in future credit quality originate credit lines to preserve financial flexibility. Furthermore, borrowers with higher FICO scores (a measure of credit risk) tend to have higher credit utilization at origination, consistent with the theoretical models[1] predicting that borrowers with lower credit quality signals preserve flexibility by utilizing a lower amount of credit at origination relative to borrowers with higher credit quality signals. Agarwal and others (2006) also found that

---

[1] See, for example, Campbell (1978); Hawkins (1982); Melnik and Plaut (1986a, 1986b); and Sofianos, Wachtel, and Melnik (1990).

2

borrower credit line utilization increases in response to drops in borrower's FICO scores, consistent with the theoretical "credit risk" prediction of Strahan (1999).

Using a sample of Spanish corporate credit lines, Jiménez, Lopez, and Saurina (2007) found that among a wide variety of loan-level, firm-level, lender-level, and macro factors that affect line utilization rates, the most important factors are a firm's default experience, the age of the credit line, and the length of the banking relationship. In particular, firms that default on their credit lines during the sample period have significantly higher line utilization rates, and these rates increase as the default year approaches. In addition, the age of the credit line and the length of the banking relationship are negatively related to utilization rate.

The empirical findings of Agarwal and others (2006) and Jiménez and others (2007) may have some implications for exposure at default (EAD) under the Basel II Capital Accord. Since credit line utilization increases significantly as borrower credit quality deteriorates, the amount outstanding might become significantly higher in the event of default, resulting in an EAD much higher than outstanding at the time of capital calculation. In other words, without considering the correlation between the borrower's probability of default and the corresponding EAD, economic capital models may underestimate the impact of credit losses. It is also necessary to evaluate revolving retail exposures during downturn periods when the credit quality of many borrowers is deteriorating and aggregate default rates are significantly higher than average.

However, it is not clear from Agarwal and others (2006) and Jiménez and others (2007) whether the increase in credit line utilization as borrower credit quality deteriorates is caused mainly by an increase in drawn amount by the borrower or, rather, a cutback of the credit line by the lender.[2] On one hand, as borrowers approach default, their financial conditions deteriorate and they are likely to tap the undrawn line as a source of additional funds, resulting in higher EAD. On the other hand, lenders may cut back credit lines to reduce potential losses if they observe deterioration of borrower credit quality[3]; as a result, higher credit utilization does not necessarily imply proportional increase in EAD.

As illustrated in figure 1, the behavior of both borrowers and lenders while they "race to default" jointly determines EAD. Under scenario A, the lender does not cut back the credit line, the initial utilization is 50 percent ($500 out of $1,000), utilization at default increases by 20 percentage points to 70 percent ($700 out of $1,000), and EAD is $700. Under scenario B, the borrower exhibits the same drawdown behavior; however, the lender quickly reduces the credit line to $600 in observation of the deteriorating credit quality of the borrower. As a result, under scenario B, although utilization at default is 100 percent (which is higher than under scenario A), the EAD is only $600 (less than the $700 under scenario A). To date, there is no empirical study that shows whether and how often banks cut back lines on revolving retail credits, and whether the "race to default" differs on accounts of different credit constraint and delinquency status. Our empirical analysis in section 3 sheds light on this.

---

[2] Cardholder agreement usually states that the lender can change account terms, such as credit limit, at the lender's discretion at any time as long as a written advance notice is provided to the cardholder.

[3] This is supported by Sufi (2009) who finds that the supply of lines of credit to corporate borrowers by banks is particularly sensitive to the borrower's profitability. Even among borrowers who have access to a bank line of credit, banks employ strict covenants on profitability, and the borrower loses access to the unused portion of the line of credit when it defaults on covenants, a situation largely caused by a drop in profitability. Consequently, low-profitability firms often hold larger cash balances in their liquidity management strategies than do high-profitability firms.

This study focuses on EAD, one of the key risk parameters in Basel II minimum risk-based capital requirements for credit risk. EAD is a bank's expected gross dollar exposure (including net accrued but unpaid interest and fees) for a facility upon the borrower's default. For fixed exposures, such as bullet or term loans, EAD is simply the amount outstanding at the time of capital calculation (plus accrued but unpaid interest and fees).[4] For variable exposures, such as lines of credit, EAD is the current outstanding plus an estimate of additional drawdowns and accrued but unpaid interest and fees up to the time of default.

To quantify EAD, banks can estimate possible increases in exposures, which consist of additional drawdowns plus net accrued but unpaid interest and fees between the time of capital calculation and a potential default by the borrower over a fixed horizon—for example, one year. Increases in exposure from the time of capital calculation to the time of default as a percent of undrawn amount at the time of capital calculation is often referred to as loan equivalent (or LEQ) by the industry. EAD can then be estimated as the current outstanding balance plus the estimated LEQ times the current undrawn, i.e., EAD($) = outstanding ($) + LEQ x [credit line ($)–outstanding($)]. In figure 1, LEQs of the defaulted loan in scenarios A and B are 40 percent and 20 percent, respectively, whereas the line utilization rates at default in scenarios A and B are 70 percent and 100 percent, respectively.

Besides LEQ, alternative approaches, such as credit conversion factor (CCF) and EAD factor (or EADF), can also be used to estimate EAD. CCF is the exposure at default

---

[4] For amortizing loans, it is possible that the amount outstanding at default may be less than the amount outstanding at the time of capital calculation if the payment received is more than the net accrued but unpaid interest and fees. However, under the U.S. Basel II Final Rule, EAD cannot be less than the amount of outstanding balance at time of capital calculation.

as a percentage of the outstanding balance at the time of capital calculation, whereas EADF is the exposure at default as a percentage of the credit line at the time of capital calculation. The CCF estimation does not incorporate information on the credit line, and EADF does not incorporate information about the outstanding balance at the time of capital calculation. LEQ, on the other hand, incorporates both pieces of information, and therefore has the potential to provide the most accurate estimation of EAD. However, when a consumer maxes out the credit line (has zero undrawn), LEQ is not defined. Also when the borrower is getting close to maxing out the credit line, with a small undrawn amount, LEQ can be highly unstable even though it is defined. In this case, CCF and EADF can be used to estimate EAD instead. As such, while our empirical modeling and analysis mainly focuses on LEQ for accounts with undrawn amounts of more than $50, we also quantify CCF and EADF when accounts have zero or very small (<$50) undrawn lines or when accounts are closed or over limit.

In the new Basel II capital framework, probability of default (PD), loss given default (LGD), and exposure at default (EAD) are the key risk parameters that jointly determine the minimum credit risk capital required to cover unexpected credit losses of financial institutions. Thanks to credit scoring introduced in the 1980s and widely adopted in the mid-1990s, factors driving PD of retail credit exposures have been fairly well studied and understood. Financial institutions have commonly used PD models in underwriting and account management of retail credits. While there are few but increasing numbers of published studies on retail LGD, as surveyed in Qi and Yang (2009), we have not seen any published studies focusing on retail EAD, although there are very few empirical studies on wholesale EAD, as surveyed here.

In their technical appendix, Asarnow and Marker (1995) present some wholesale EAD analysis based on a small sample of 50 large corporate loans at Citibank from 1988 to 1993. They find that while lower credit quality borrowers have higher line utilization, they appear to have lower LEQ. Higher-quality borrowers may have higher LEQ because they are subject to fewer restrictions and covenants and less strict monitoring, and in times of trouble they can draw down available credit without interference from the bank. The Chase study by Araten and Jacobs (2001) uses a much larger sample (408 defaulted facilities observed at various times) from 1995 to 2000. They find that LEQ generally decreases with increasing risk, but results are not robust. They also find that LEQ is not differentiated by lending organization (e.g., middle market vs. large corporate), commitment type, commitment size, domestic vs. foreign, or industry. Moral (2006) provides a survey of pros and cons of various EAD estimation methods and illustrates these points using a set of defaulted facilities from a small and medium enterprise (SME) portfolio. Jacobs (2008) expands the previous empirical works on wholesale EAD by considering additional risk drivers, various measures of EAD risk, and in-sample and out-of-sample performance of alternative statistical models using updated and expanded data on 3,886 defaulted instruments for 683 borrowers from 1985 to 2007.

Most of the advanced IRB (internal-ratings-based) banks in the U.S. banking industry do not have EAD models or develop EAD segmentation using EAD-specific risk drivers, and common industry practice is to use average LEQ or CCF for each retail product or for each PD segment. Since little is known about retail EAD and its risk drivers, and the U.S. Basel II Final Rule is not specific about the approach to EAD, we try to fill this gap in the academic literature and in industry practices. To summarize our major findings up front, we use a large national sample of unsecured credit card defaults and find that a set of variables consisting of borrower attributes, account information variables, and macro factors are significant drivers of EAD. Models incorporating these factors show better predictive accuracy. We also find that in the "race to default," borrowers are more likely to draw down additional funds but lenders rarely cut back credit limits, although lenders make it less easy to draw down additional funds as borrowers become more severely delinquent. The rest of the paper is organized as follows: Data description and summary statistics are provided in section 2. The dynamic behavior of borrowers and lenders as the borrowers approach default is analyzed in section 3. Correlation analysis between key variables is provided in section 4. Results of regression analysis and predictive accuracy of alternative models are reported in sections 5 and 6, respectively. Conclusions are drawn in section 7.

2. Data Description and Summary Statistics

Data used for this study are obtained from the OCC Consumer Credit Database (CCDB). CCDB is a large multiyear extract of both tradeline (account) and summary information for individual consumers from one of the three U.S. national credit bureaus. CCDB covers more than 1 million consumers and contains 10–15 million tradelines each year from 1999 to 2008.

In this study, we focus on credit cards, the largest component of revolving retail credit for most if not all advanced IRB banks in the United States. According to a report by R.K. Hammer Investment Bankers, credit cards accounted for 6.9 percent of bank assets and 16 percent of bank earnings in 2007 and in each of the last five years, and the contribution to bank earnings by credit card businesses has been at least twice as large as the percentage of assets they represent.[5] Another reason for our focus on credit cards is that in CCDB, credit cards have the largest number of defaults compared with other revolving retail credit products such as revolving charge accounts, check credit or lines of credit, secured credit cards, combined credit plans, secured credit lines, or home equity lines of credit. We exclude secured credit cards because in the United States, credit card accounts are predominantly unsecured and, more important, secured credit card accounts behave very differently in drawdown patterns as the borrowers approach default.

We use the Basel II definition of default; that is, a credit card account is considered defaulted if it is 180 days past due or has been partially or fully charged off. A fixed horizon of one year is used to calculate LEQ, CCF, and EADF. Account and consumer information one year prior to default is used to explain the variations in LEQ. Although there are more than 1 million credit card defaults in CCDB, we can trace the account and consumer information one year prior to default for only 152,657 defaults.[6] The LEQ, CCF, and EADF of these accounts are reported in table 1, which shows huge variation in all three EAD measures, especially LEQ. LEQ is calculated for 141,069 defaulted accounts that had nonzero undrawn amounts, and it ranges from –503,500 percent to 650,100 percent, with a mean of 166 percent, a median of 21 percent, and a standard deviation of 6,826 percent.

A little over 40 percent (or 61,494 out of 152,657) of all the defaulted accounts in our sample were either closed or over the credit limit one year prior to default. Since lenders usually do not allow these accounts to draw additional funds, LEQ tends to be

---

[5] Harry Terris, "Cards Contributing More Bank Income," *American Banker*, April 21, 2008.

[6] In CCDB, balance and consumer attributes are updated only as of June 30 each year, but default can occur any time in the year. Consequently, account and consumer attributes one year prior to default date cannot be obtained for many defaults.

very small if not zero or negative, as shown in table 1. These accounts are analyzed

separately, as they would cause a downward bias in EAD estimates if they were included

in the sample. For closed accounts, the mean LEQ, CCF, and EADF are 67 percent, 121

percent, and 124 percent, respectively, and the maxima are 162,600 percent, 42,700

percent, and 13,120 percent, respectively. This indicates that it is still possible for some

closed accounts to have balance increases that might not be totally attributed to accrued

and unpaid interests and fees. About one in four of the 3,982 closed accounts experienced

balance increases.

The mean and 25th percentile CCF for over-limit accounts are greater than 100

percent, and about 88.2 percent of the 57,512 over-limit accounts experienced balance

increases as they approached default. Therefore, there is still exposure risk on the closed

or over-limit accounts, and it is not appropriate to automatically assume LEQ=0 on these

accounts. This has important implications for Basel II LEQ estimation. The negative LEQ

occurs either when the balance amount increases on over-limit accounts or when the

balance amount decreases on under-limit accounts. In our sample, 41.6 percent of the

141,069 defaults with nonzero undrawn amounts show negative LEQs, of which 86.3

percent is due to an over limit (or negative undrawn amount) instead of balance

decreases; for those accounts, CCF or EADF rather than LEQ should be used to quantify

EAD. Banks often floor negative LEQ at zero regardless of the reasons for negative LEQ.

As we show here, depending on the cause of the negative LEQ, blindly setting an LEQ

floor of zero for negative LEQ observations is not necessarily conservative.

In table 2, we take the 93,027 open accounts that are not over limit, divide them

into three groups based on undrawn amounts—equals to $0, greater than $0 but less than or equal to $50, and greater than $50—and then report the descriptive statistics of each group. For the 11,056 accounts with zero undrawn amounts one year prior to default, LEQ is undefined, the average and median CCF are 196 percent and 136 percent, respectively, and the EADF is identical to CCF (the account balance was equal to the credit limit for these borrowers one year prior to default). For the 15,945 accounts with greater than $0 but less than or equal to $50, the mean and median CCF and EADF are all above 150 percent, whereas the LEQ swings wildly from –426,575 percent to 381,600 percent, with a mean of 4,262 percent and median of 1,888 percent. The mean and median LEQ are 242 percent and 151 percent, respectively, for the 66,026 open accounts with undrawn amounts greater than $50. The group with more than $50 undrawn lines one year prior to default also has the highest mean and median EAD and the lowest line utilization rate at default (Util).

Table 2 also shows the summary statistics of the borrower characteristics one year prior to default. Variable definitions are shown in the appendix. The group with higher undrawn amounts seems to have higher credit scores (Score0), higher aggregate balances (AggCardBal0), and lower aggregate line utilization (AggCardUtil0), compared with the groups with lower undrawn amounts; the group with the highest undrawn amount also has the highest average aggregate home equity balance (AggHEBal0). In terms of individual account information, table 2 shows that one year prior to default, the group with higher undrawn amounts is associated with a lower individual account credit limit utilization rate (Util0); the group with the largest undrawn amount tends to have the most number of years since the account opened (Age0), the highest credit limit (Cred_Amt0) and credit balance (Bal_Amt0), the largest undrawn amount

11

(Undrn_Amt0), the largest payment amount (Payment_Amt0), and the highest balance amount (High_Bal0) and chargeoff amount (Chgoff_Amt0).

The accounts with no more than $50 undrawn amounts one year prior to default show a large variation in EAD measures (LEQ, CCF, and EADF), but represent less than 30 percent of the total number and a little over 16 percent of total EAD of open accounts that are at or under limit. Moreover, due to the very small undrawn amounts (less than $50), a small change in balance will likely result in a huge LEQ. As such, our empirical modeling and analysis focuses only on the subsample of 66,026 accounts that are open and have undrawn amounts greater than $50.

Late or missing payments on an account signal higher risk, which could prompt lenders to block the borrower's attempt to draw additional amounts. Thus, current accounts one year prior to default are riskier than delinquent accounts in terms of elevated drawdown tendency. This is clearly shown in table 3. For the 54,955 accounts that were current one year prior to default, the mean, median, 25th percentile, and 75th percentile LEQ, CCF, and EADF are all higher than those of the 11,071 accounts that were delinquent one year prior to default. Accounts that were current one year prior to default also tend to show a larger EAD and higher line utilization as they approach default, compared with accounts that were delinquent one year prior to default.[7] Not surprisingly, accounts that were current one year prior to default show higher credit scores (Score0), larger aggregate bankcard balances (AggCardBal0), higher aggregate line utilization rates (AggCardUtil0), and larger aggregate open home equity balances (AggHEBal0) than their delinquent counterparts one year prior to default. Delinquent

---

[7] Table 5 in section 3 also shows that the current accounts experience larger increases in credit limit and larger increases in balances compared with the delinquent accounts.

accounts tend to have slightly higher line utilization rates, longer times since the account opened, and higher past due and payment amounts than current accounts.

Lenders may reduce their exposure by lowering loan commitments, lines of credit, or credit card limits in periods of economic downturn, which might result in lower downturn EAD estimates. On the other hand, borrowers facing financial constraints during an economic downturn may need to draw down more funds, resulting in higher downturn EAD estimates. To investigate whether and how EAD may differ under economic downturn conditions, we tracked quarterly default rates in all qualified revolving exposures (QREs) in our sample from 1998Q3 to 2008Q2. Following the Basel II definition, QRE includes revolving charge accounts, check credits or lines of credit, credit cards, and combined revolving credit plans, all with credit limits of less than $100,000. As we did with credit cards, we used the Basel II definition of default for QRE—i.e., an account is considered defaulted if it is 180 days past due or has been partially or fully charged off. The quarterly default rate is calculated as the total number of accounts defaulted in a quarter as a percentage of total number of nondefaulted accounts at the beginning of the quarter. Figure 2 shows quarterly QRE default rates and the number of QRE defaults. While the peaks of QRE default rates in the periods of 2002–2003 and 2007–2008 were caused by downturn economic conditions, the peak in 2005Q2 was caused by the rush to file for bankruptcy before the Bankruptcy Abuse Prevention and Consumer Protection (BAPCP) Act of 2005 became effective in October 2005. The BAPCP Act makes it harder for borrowers to get their debt discharged.

To capture the effect of economic downturn conditions on EAD, we plotted the annual QRE default rates and annual average EADF from 1999 to 2008 in figure 3.

Figure 3 shows that 2002 has the second-highest annual QRE default rate of 3.02 percent and the highest annual average EADF of 181 percent for all unsecured credit card defaults in our sample, suggesting a higher EAD in downturn economic conditions. On the contrary, 2008 has the highest annual QRE default rate of 3.93 percent but the lowest average EADF of 130 percent throughout the entire sample period of 1999–2008, which may suggest a lower EAD in the recent economic downturn resulting from cutbacks of credit card limits by lenders. This is supported in figure 4, which shows annual QRE default rates, credit limit cutback probability, and credit limit increase probability. As can be seen from figure 4, compared with the 2002–2003 downturn, the recent downturn shows a much lower probability of credit limit increases (12 percent vs. 25 percent) but a much higher probability of credit limit cutbacks (21 percent vs. 7 percent). Our empirical analysis in sections 3–5 sheds more light on this.

3.   Who Are More Active in the "Race to Default": the Borrowers or the Lenders?

As discussed in section 1, the EAD for revolving exposures is determined by the outcome of the "race to default" by the borrowers and the lenders as the borrowers approach default. The more the borrowers draw down the unused credit limit and the less the lenders cut back the credit limit, the higher the EAD. To date, we have not seen published studies that show whether the borrowers or the lenders are more active as they "race to default," and whether the race differs depending on credit constraint and delinquency status.

Table 4 shows the frequency and magnitude of credit limit cutbacks and increases, and balance increases every three months from one year prior to default to three months prior to default. Since CCDB data are sampled annually, while we have

152,657 observations for 12 months prior to default, there are fewer observations within a year, ranging from 38,522 nine months prior to default to 20,136 three months prior to default. Nevertheless, these are sufficient for our purpose.

Table 4 shows that lenders cut back credit limits much less often than they increase credit limits, and balance amounts often increase as borrowers approach default. From one year prior to default to default, only 7.9 percent of the 152,657 defaulted credit card accounts in our sample experienced credit limit cutbacks, whereas 29.6 percent of them had credit limit increases and around 88.4 percent of them showed higher balances. From nine, six, and three months prior to default to default, only 6.9 percent, 6.3 percent, and 5.1 percent of the total number of defaulted accounts experienced cutbacks in credit limits; whereas 37.5 percent, 14.9 percent, and 13.2 percent of them had credit limit increases; and 81.2 percent, 72.6 percent, and 65.3 percent showed balance increases.

Table 4 also shows that on average, credit limits increased by 24.9 percent, 28.9 percent, 7.8 percent, and 4.2 percent from one year, nine months, six months, and three months prior to default to default, although the median increase in credit limit was 0 percent at all four time horizons. Meanwhile, on average, balance amounts increased by 144.2 percent, 105.3 percent, 33.5 percent, and 3.3 percent from one year, nine months, six months, and three months prior to default to default; and the median increases in balance amounts are 31.0 percent, 30.0 percent, 13.9 percent, and 4.7 percent at the four respective horizons. While in table 4 we do observe consistent decreases in LEQ, CCF, and EADF as time to default decreases, on average, the outstanding balances continue to grow, although at a slower rate as the default time gets nearer.

Table 5 reports the changes in credit limit and balance for open accounts with different undrawn amounts and delinquency status. We find that credit limit reduction is the least likely (5.6 percent probability) among accounts that have undrawn amounts above $0 but not more than $50, compared with open accounts that have either $0 or more than $50 undrawn amounts, for which the probability of credit limit reduction is 16.5 percent and 12.4 percent, respectively. More important, the probabilities of credit limit increases are 79.2 percent, 41.0 percent and 26.1 percent, respectively, for open accounts that have $0, greater than $0 but less than $50, and more than $50 undrawn amounts; and on average credit limits increase by 86 percent, 44 percent, and 11.5 percent, respectively, for these three undrawn amount groups, suggesting that the more the accounts are credit constrained, the more likely the increase in credit limit and the larger the percentage increase in the size of the credit limit. Meanwhile, the probabilities of balance increases for these three groups are 93.4 percent, 92.1 percent, and 88.5 percent, respectively; and their balances increase by 96.2 percent, 78.1 percent, and 273.4 percent, respectively, from one year prior to default to the time of default. Therefore, there is evidence that the supply of credit in existing accounts is driven by demand and, as borrowers approach default, it is often the borrowers rather than the lenders who take actions during the "race to default."

Table 5 also shows that among those open accounts with more than $50 undrawn, the frequency and magnitude of credit limit increases and balance increases are much lower for delinquent accounts than for current accounts. This is consistent with common account management practices of lenders who usually consider delinquency as a signal to take credit risk reduction actions. The last panel of table 5 shows the change in credit limits and balances for open and delinquent accounts with more than $50 undrawn across delinquency buckets of one, two, three, four, and five months. Both the probability of credit limit increases and the probability of balance increases decline as the accounts move down the delinquency buckets, as do the percentage increase in credit limits and the percentage increase in balance amounts. This may suggest that although it is still possible for delinquent borrowers to continue borrowing, lenders make it less easy to do so as borrowers become more severely delinquent.

In summary, we find evidence that borrowers are more likely to draw down additional funds, but lenders infrequently cut back credit limits and sometimes raise credit limits (although less frequently as borrowers approach default).[8] On average, we see outstanding balances continue to grow and credit limits continue to increase, although at a slower rate as the default time gets nearer. Analyzing credit limits for accounts with different undrawn amounts reveals that the more the account is credit constrained, the more likely it will get an increase in credit limit and the larger the percentage increase in credit limit, coupled with sizable balance increases across the board. This suggests that the supply of credit is largely driven by demand and, as borrowers approach default, it is often the borrowers instead of the lenders who take actions. Analysis in this section also shows that lenders do consider delinquency as a signal to take credit risk mitigation actions. Although it is still possible for delinquent borrowers to continue borrowing, lenders make it less easy to do so as borrowers become more severely delinquent.

---

[8] Annual percentage rate (APR) is routinely set to a higher penalty rate if an account becomes delinquent or if the credit score of the cardholder drops to a certain level (due to delinquency or default on the cardholder's other debt obligations). This may partly explain why card issuers do not usually cut back credit limit.

4. Correlation Analysis

This section analyzes pairwise correlations to identify potential drivers of LEQ for open accounts with undrawn amounts greater than $50. The results for the current and delinquent accounts can be found in tables 6 and 7, respectively. Boldface numbers are statistically significant at the 5 percent level, and numbers underlined are significant at the 10 percent level.

Table 6 shows that EAD is positively correlated with LEQ, as expected. Among all borrower and account characteristics, the dummy variable indicating accounts with utilization rate greater than 95 percent (Util0_95) one year prior to default shows the highest positive correlation (0.212) with LEQ, and the account credit limit utilization rate one year prior to default (Util0) has the second-highest positive correlation (0.173) with LEQ. Other variables that show significant positive correlation with LEQ include AggCardUtil0, payment amount, Inq0, and balance amount, all observed one year prior to default. Among borrower and account characteristics that show significant negative correlation with LEQ, credit score, years since account open, and credit limit show larger impact than the dummy for accounts with 0 utilization rate, NumAcnt0, chargeoff amount, high balance amount, amount past due, and AggHEBal0. Among the macro factors, QRE_DftRate0 is significantly positively correlated with LEQ, Rush_to_File is positively correlated with LEQ but is not statistically significant, and Post_BAPCP is significantly correlated with LEQ at the 10 percent level.

Several high pairwise correlations among the account, borrower, and environmental variables are worth noting in table 6. One year prior to default, both high balance amount and payment amount are highly correlated with account balance amount, credit limit, and AggCardBal0, and balance amount is highly correlated with credit limit, AggCardBal0, and account credit limit utilization rate.[9] Account credit limit utilization is also positively correlated with AggCardUtil0. Just as expected, the borrower's aggregate credit line utilization rate (AggCardUtil0) is negatively correlated with the borrower's credit score.

For delinquent accounts, table 7 shows that EAD is positively correlated with LEQ, as expected. Similar to current accounts, among all borrower and account characteristics, Util0_95 has the highest positive correlation (0.166) with LEQ; Util0 has the second-highest positive correlation (0.165) with LEQ; and AggCardUtil0, AggCardBal0, and payment amount are also significantly positively correlated with LEQ for delinquent accounts. Unlike current accounts, for delinquent accounts, Inq0 and balance amount are no longer significant positively correlated with LEQ. Seven variables are significantly negatively correlated LEQ, some of which are the same variables as in table 6 for current accounts, such as years since account open, credit score, credit limit, high balance amount, and NumAcnt0. Number of months past due (Dlq0) is unique to delinquent accounts and is negatively correlated with LEQ, as expected. It is worth noting that for delinquent accounts Post_BAPCP is significantly negatively correlated with LEQ, while it is marginally significantly correlated with LEQ for current accounts. Other variables (e.g., chargeoff amount, Inq0, AggHEBal0) were negatively correlated

---

[9] Since credit limit could reveal a lender's assessment of a borrower's creditworthiness or profitability, at certain times (mostly in the 1990s), lenders did not report credit limit to the credit bureau or report the high balance as the credit limit. From 1999 to 2008, in CCDB, around 5 percent of 45,694,621 card years have unknown credit limit, and around 16.5 percent of card years have equal credit limit and high balance. There has been a steady and obvious improvement in credit limit reporting practice, with the probability of unreported credit limits dropping from 21 percent in 1999 to 0.5 percent in 2008, and the probability of equal credit limit and high balance decreasing from 22 percent in 1999 to 7.5 percent in 2008. The high correlation of 0.902 between credit limit and high balance may be partly caused by the credit limit reporting practice of lenders.

with LEQ for current accounts; they are no longer so with delinquent accounts. As in current accounts, for delinquent accounts, QRE_DftRate0 is positively correlated with LEQ and Post_BAPCP is negatively correlated with LEQ.

Table 7 also shows several high pairwise correlations among the account, borrower, and environmental variables for delinquent accounts. Just as in current accounts, one year prior to default, both high balance amounts and payment amounts are highly correlated with account balance amounts, credit limits, and AggCardBal0, and balance amounts are highly correlated with credit limit, AggCardBal0, and account credit limit utilization rate for delinquent accounts.[10] In addition, balance amount and past due amount are highly correlated with credit limit. Account credit limit utilization is also positively correlated with AggCardUtil0. Just as expected, AggCardUtil0 is negatively correlated with the borrower's credit score.

5. Regression Analysis

As explained in section 2, our regression analysis is conducted for data on open accounts with undrawn amounts greater than $50, which represent more than 70 percent of the total number (but comprise about 84 percent of the total exposure amount) of all open accounts that are not over limit in our sample. Sample period is from 1999 to 2006, which includes defaults that occurred between July 1, 1998, and June 30, 2006. The dependent variable is LEQ and the explanatory variables include various borrower, account, and macro variables. One significant data challenge is the outliers. Even for this subset of the open accounts with more than $50 undrawn, there are still outliers, and

---

[10] Again, the high correlation of 0.889 between credit limit and high balance may be partly caused by lenders' credit limit reporting practices. See footnote 9 for more detail.

some of these outliers are many standard deviations away from the mean. For example, the maximum LEQ of 51,113 percent for current accounts is more than 65 standard deviations away from the mean of 262 percent, whereas the minimum LEQ of –33,789 percent is more than 43 standard deviations away from the mean. Different treatments of these outliers may significantly impact the regression results; thus, we report regression results including and excluding outliers.[11]

The results for current and delinquent accounts are shown in tables 8 and 9, respectively. Excluding the outliers does not seem to alter the signs and magnitudes for most parameters, but the goodness of fit has been substantially improved. To avoid data-snooping bias, we show both the regression results with all candidate variables included and the regression results from stepwise regression, which is a modified forward-selection procedure (variables already in the model do not necessarily stay there).[12] As can be seen from both tables 8 and 9, the signs and magnitudes of nearly all parameters as well as the adjusted R^2 stay largely the same; therefore, our discussion of empirical results in these tables is based only on the stepwise regression results. Because of space constraints, our discussion of empirical results below are based primarily on the stepwise regression excluding the outliers.[13]

---

[11] Visual inspection of the residual plot shows that residual value of 2,000 percent is a reasonably good threshold for outliers. This threshold is fewer than 3 standard deviations away from the mean for current accounts and fewer than 4 standard deviations away from the mean for delinquent accounts.

[12] As with forward selection, variables with the F statistic above a chosen level for entering are added one by one to the model. After a variable is added, however, the stepwise method looks at all the variables already included in the model and deletes any variable that does not produce an F statistic significant at the chosen level for staying. The stepwise process ends when none of the variables outside the model has an F statistic significant at the chosen level for entering and every variable in the model is significant at the chosen level for staying, or when the variable to be added to the model is the one just deleted from it.

[13] Residual plots do not show an obvious relationship between residual and predicted LEQ. Residual histograms are bell shaped and appear to be normal. There is no significant residual autocorrelation based on the Durbin-Watson test.

For the 36,753 accounts that were open and current one year prior to default with undrawn amounts greater than $50, table 8 shows that borrower attributes (Score0, AggCardBal0, AggCardUtil0, Inq0, and NumAcnt0), account characteristics (Util0, Age0, Bal_Amt0, Pastdue_Amt0, Chgoff_Amt0), and the quarterly default rate of all QREs and Post_BAPCP are significant risk drivers of LEQ. First, among the borrower attributes, the higher the credit score, the larger the aggregate balance of all open bankcards, the larger the total number of open retail tradelines, the lower the LEQ, and thus the smaller the EAD; on the other hand, the higher the aggregate utilization of all open bankcards and the larger the number of inquiries within the past six months, the higher the LEQ and thus the larger the EAD. Second, among the account characteristics, the number of years since the account opened, account balance, amount past due, and chargeoff amount are negatively related to LEQ, and account credit limit utilization (especially for accounts with zero or greater than 95 percent utilization rate) is significantly positively related to LEQ. Third, it is important to note that the quarterly default rate of all qualifying revolving exposures in our database is significantly positively related to LEQ, suggesting that a downturn LEQ is necessary, as periods with higher-than-average QRE default rates are likely to have higher LEQ and thus larger EAD. Last, the implementation of the BAPCP Act is associated with lower LEQ, everything else being equal.

Table 9 shows that the LEQ risk drivers are somewhat different for the 7,019 accounts that were open but delinquent one year prior to default with undrawn amounts greater than $50, compared with those for accounts that were open and current one year prior to default. Several risk drivers—consumer credit score, aggregate balance for open bankcards, number of inquiries, total number of open retail tradelines, and chargeoff amount—are no longer significant. The credit score is insignificant, as expected, because delinquent borrowers should all have fairly low scores anyway. Several risk drivers—credit limit and Rush_to_File—are now significant. The delinquency status indicators are all negatively correlated and highly significant—the more severely delinquent, the less likely the borrowers were able to draw additional funds, and thus the lower the LEQ. This indicates that lenders do follow risk-based account management strategies (more discussion on this is provided in section 3). Post_BAPCP is negatively correlated and highly significant, while the "Rush-to-File" dummy is significantly positively correlated, indicating that delinquent borrowers not only rushed to file bankruptcy but also engaged in a "rush to draw down" before the act's implementation in October 2005 (but not after). The LEQ significantly dropped after the implementation of BAPCP, which suggests that the law seems to have met the goal it set out to achieve. On the contrary, for accounts that were current one year prior to default, there were no significant increases in drawdown behavior when outliers were excluded before the implementation of BAPCP Act, but there were significant decreases in LEQ afterward.

6. Predictive Accuracy of Alternative EAD/LEQ Models

Most of the advanced IRB banks in the United States do not develop EAD/LEQ segmentation or EAD/LEQ models using EAD-specific risk drivers. They often estimate LEQ or CCF by taking an average for each retail PD segment or for each retail product, such as average LEQ or CCF for credit cards, home equity lines of credit, etc. In the section, we compare the predictive accuracy of alternative LEQ models and commonly used methods in the industry for both current and delinquent accounts one year prior to default, as shown in table 10.[14]

In addition to the four models reported in tables 8 and 9, we also include one alternative regression model (Model 5), in which LEQ is censored following a common industry practice, i.e., negative LEQ values were set to zero and LEQ values above 100 percent were set to 100 percent. Root mean squared error (RMSE) of the common industry practice of average LEQ from censored and raw data is also reported in table 10. All models and averages were estimated based on samples from file years 1999 to 2006, which contain defaults that occurred from July 1, 1998, to June 30, 2006. The estimated models and averages were then used to generate out-of-sample predictions of LEQ for file years 2007 to 2008, which contain defaults that occurred from July 1, 2006, to June 30, 2008.

A few observations can be made from table 10. First, across all models and methods, the out-of-sample RMSE is smaller than the in-sample RMSE for current accounts, whereas the opposite is true for delinquent accounts. Second, models 1–4 show similar predictive accuracy both in and out of sample, although models 1 and 3, where all observations were included, show slightly smaller in-sample RMSE but slightly higher out-of-sample RMSE than models 2 and 4, where outliers were excluded. Stepwise regression and regression that includes all candidate variables do not make a difference in terms of predictive accuracy. Third, LEQ censoring results in higher RMSE both in and out of sample, for both current and delinquent accounts, and for both regression model and sample average LEQ. Finally, compared with the three common industry practices,

---

[14] We also calculated RMSE of EAD using alternative LEQ models and methods, and found that the relative performance of alternative LEQ models based on RMSE of EAD stays the same as that based on RMSE of LEQ. Therefore RMSE of EAD is not reported in table 10.

models 1–4 show better predictive accuracy both in and out of sample for current accounts, and better predictive accuracy in sample for delinquent accounts. Models 2 and 4 also have better predictive accuracy out of sample for delinquent accounts, whereas models 1 and 3 show similar RMSE compared with the three industry practices.

Overall, we find that among alternative EAD/LEQ models and approaches investigated in this study, models that make use of LEQ-specific risk drivers show better predictive accuracy. Excluding outliers helps improve out-of-sample forecasting accuracy, but LEQ censoring results in poorer predictive accuracy both in and out of sample.

7. Conclusions

Quantitative modeling and analysis of EAD for retail exposures is lagging in both industry practices and academic literature, compared with other risk parameters (PD and LGD) required for the Basel II regulatory capital framework. The U.S. Basel II Final Rule is not specific about the approach to EAD and therefore leaves banks with a wide range of possibilities. It is not clear which borrower characteristics, account information, and macro factors are important determinants of EAD, and there is no study that compares the predictive accuracy of alternative EAD models and methods. Academic literature on increases in credit line utilization as borrower credit quality deteriorates does not have clear implication for EAD, as utilization could increase either by additional drawdown of funds by the borrower or by credit line cutbacks by the lender. The present study tries to address these issues. Using a large sample of unsecured credit card defaults that contain both borrower attributes and account information, we try to capture borrower

25

and lender behavior as borrowers approach default and to measure and model LEQ, a commonly used approach to estimate EAD.

Analysis of the credit limit and account balance at various times prior to default reveals that borrowers are more likely to draw down additional funds and lenders infrequently cut back credit limits and sometimes increase credit limits (although lenders are less likely to do so as borrowers approach default). On average, we see outstanding balances continue to grow and credit limits continue to increase, although at a slower rate as the default time gets nearer. Analyzing credit limits for accounts with different undrawn amounts reveals that the more the account is credit constrained, the more likely the account is getting a credit limit bump-up, and the larger the percentage increase in credit limit. Further, there are sizable balance increases across the board. This suggests that the supply of credit is largely driven by demand and, as borrowers approach default, it is often the borrowers instead of the lenders who take action. We also find that lenders do consider delinquency as a signal to take credit risk mitigation actions. Although it is still possible for delinquent borrowers to continue borrowing, lenders make it less easy to do so as borrowers become more severely delinquent.

We find that borrower attributes, such as credit score, aggregate bankcard balance, aggregate bankcard credit line utilization rate, number of recent credit inquiries, and number of open retail accounts, are significant drivers of LEQ for accounts that were current one year prior to default, but none of these is significant for accounts that were delinquent one year prior to default. Among the account information variables, we find that utilization rate (especially the higher utilization rate of 95 percent or above) is the most significant driver of LEQ for both current and delinquent accounts. Account age and balance amount are also significant for both current and delinquent accounts. Additional significant drivers for current accounts include amount past due and chargeoff amount, whereas for delinquent accounts, delinquency status and credit limit show statistical significance. Among the environmental factors we investigated, there is evidence of changing drawdown behavior before and after the implementation of Bankruptcy Abuse Prevention and Consumer Protection Act of 2005. Most important, we find the LEQ is significantly higher in periods with elevated overall QRE default rates, suggesting a significant downturn EAD effect. Among alternative EAD/LEQ models and approaches investigated in this study, models that make use of LEQ-specific risk drivers show better predictive accuracy. Excluding outliers helps improve out-of-sample forecasting accuracy, but LEQ censoring results in poorer predictive accuracy both in and out of sample.

Future work is needed to compare the forecasting accuracy of alternative EAD approaches, such as CCF or EADF, to that of the LEQ, and to investigate the performance of the cohort and fixed-horizon approaches. In addition to the one-year horizon, alternative horizons can also be tested to determine whether there is an optimal horizon that is more likely to produce the most accurate and reliable EAD estimates.

References

Agarwal, Sumit, Brent W. Ambrose, and Chunlin Liu. "Credit Lines and Credit Utilization." *Journal of Money, Credit, and Banking* 38 (2006): 1–22.

Araten, Michael, and Michael Jacobs Jr. "Loan Equivalents for Revolving Credits and Advised Lines." *The RMA Journal* (May 2001): 34–39.

Asarnow, Elliot, and James Marker. "Historical Performance of the U.S. Corporate Loan Market: 1988–1993." *Commercial Lending Review* 10, no. 2 (1995): 13–32.

Campbell, Tim S. "A Model of the Market for Lines of Credit." *Journal of Finance* 23 (1978): 231–44.

Hawkins, Gregory D. "An Analysis of Revolving Credit Arrangements." *Journal of Financial Economics* 10 (1982): 59–81.

Jacobs Jr., Michael. "An Empirical Study of Exposure at Default." OCC Working Paper. Washington, DC: Office of the Comptroller of the Currency, 2008.

Jiménez, Gabriel, Jose A. Lopez, and Jesús Saurina. "Empirical Analysis of Corporate Credit Lines." Federal Reserve Bank of San Francisco Working Paper 2007-14. San Francisco: Federal Reserve Bank of San Francisco, 2007.

Melnik, Arie, and Steven E. Plaut. "The Economics of Loan Commitment Contracts: Credit Pricing and Utilization." *Journal of Banking and Finance* 10 (1986a): 267–80.

_____. "Loan Commitment Contracts, Terms of Lending, and Credit Allocation." *Journal of Finance* 41 (1986b): 425–35.

Moral, Gregorio. "EAD Estimates for Facilities with Explicit Limits." In *The Basel II Risk Parameters: Estimation, Validation, and Stress Testing,* edited by Bernd Engelmann and Robert Rauhmeler. pp. 197-242. Berlin: Springer, 2006.

Qi, Min, and Xiaolong Yang. "Loss Given Default of High Loan-to-Value Residential Mortgages." *Journal of Banking and Finance* 33, no. 5 (2009): 788–99.

Sofianos, George, Paul Wachtel, and Arie Melnik. "Loan Commitments and Monetary Policy." *Journal of Banking and Finance* 14 (1990): 677–89.

Strahan, Philip E. "Borrower Risk and the Price and Nonprice Terms of Bank Loans." Federal Reserve Bank of New York Working Paper. New York: Federal Reserve Bank of New York, 1999.

Sufi, Amir. "Bank Lines of Credit in Corporate Finance: An Empirical Analysis." *Review of Financial Studies* 22, no. 3 (2009): 1057-1088.

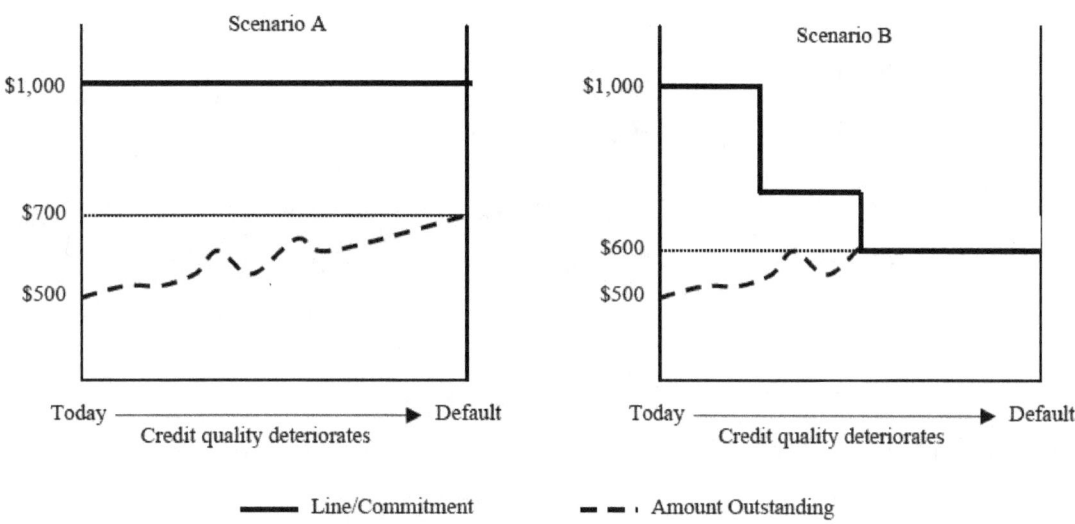

Figure 1. "Race to Default"

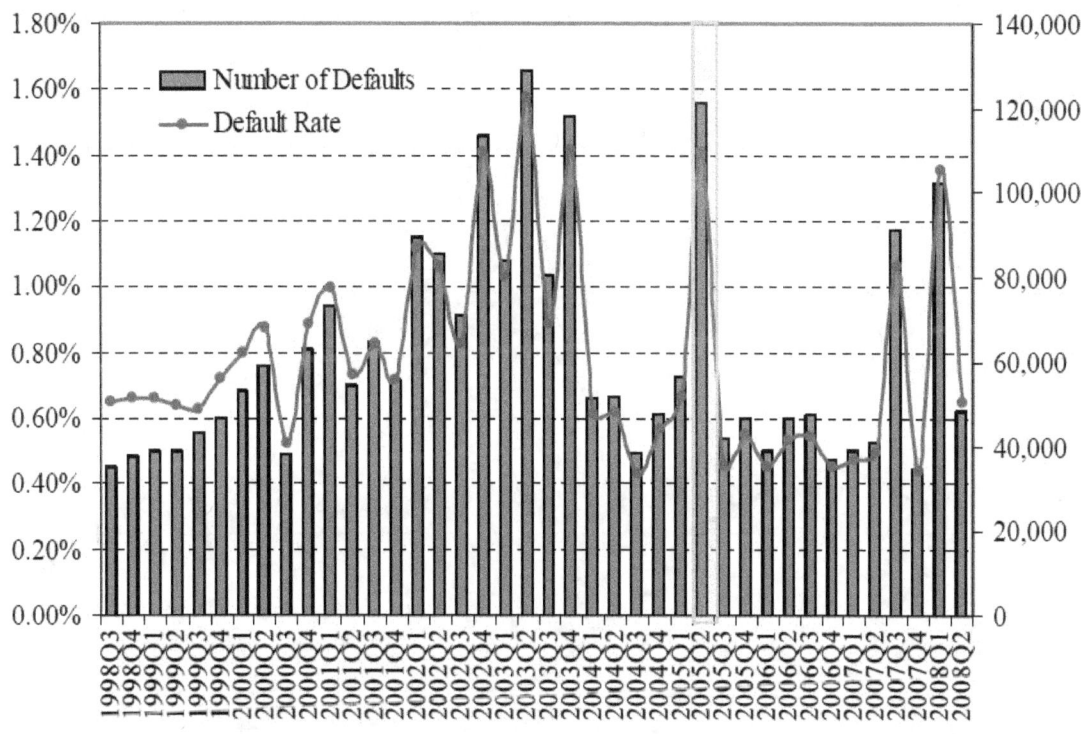

Figure 2. Quarterly QRE Default Rates and Number of QRE Defaults
(1998Q3–2008Q2)

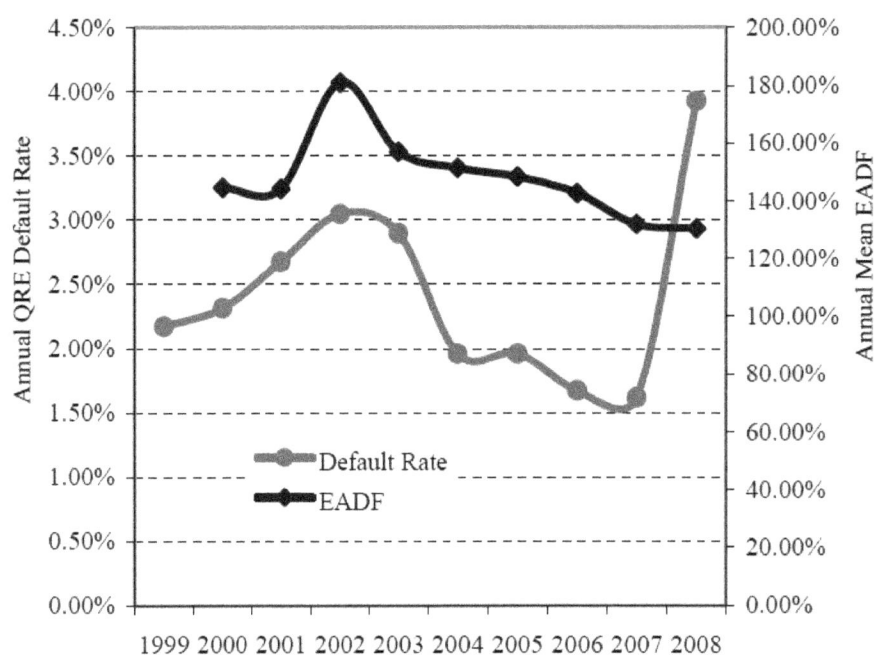

Figure 3. Annual QRE Default Rates and Average EADF of Unsecured Credit Cards (1999–2008)

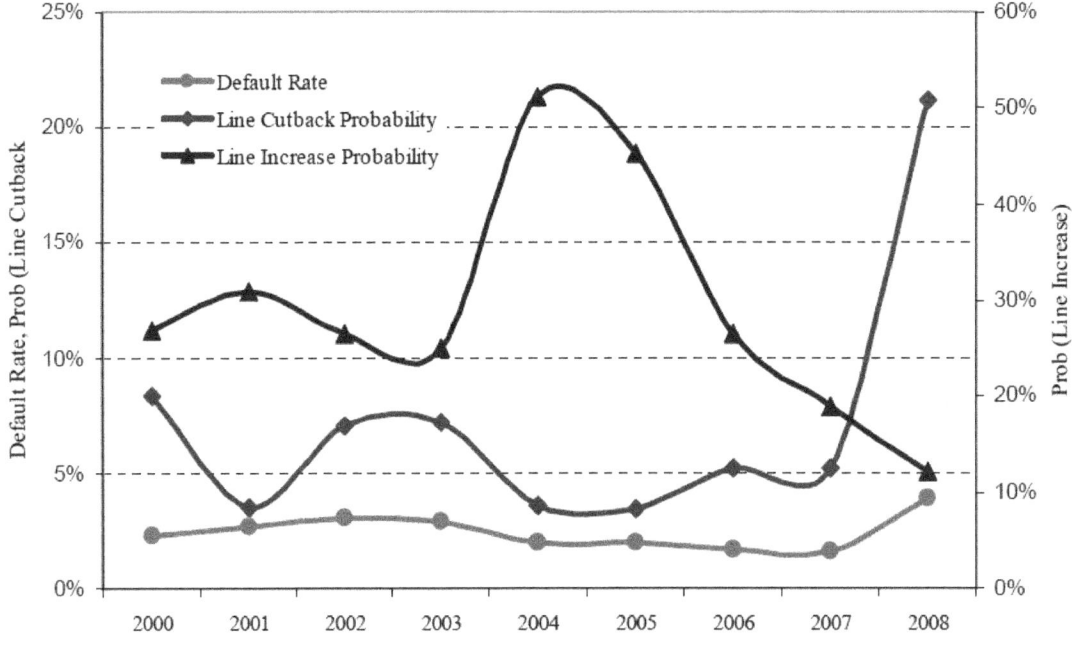

Figure 4. Annual QRE Default Rates and Probabilities of Credit Limit Increases and Cutbacks of Unsecured Credit Cards (2000–2008)

Table 1. Summary Statistics for All Types of Accounts

Variable	N	Min	Max	Mean	Std Dev	25th Pctl	Median	75th Pctl
All Accounts								
LEQ (%)	141,069	−503,500	650,100	166	6,826	−155	21	322
CCF (%)	148,786	0	1,105,233	244	3,956	112	131	167
EADF (%)	152,657	0	66,300	148	383	106	131	165
Open Accounts with Undrawn Amount ≥ $0								
LEQ (%)	81,971	−426,575	381,600	1,024	6,039	48	214	687
CCF (%)	89,896	0	1,105,233	317	5,085	117	138	189
EADF (%)	93,027	0	51,113	131	369	92	120	149
Closed Accounts								
LEQ (%)	3,450	−35,254	162,600	67	2,902	0	0	0
CCF (%)	3,242	0	42,700	121	773	100	100	100
EADF (%)	3,982	0	13,120	124	237	79	113	150
Over-limit Accounts								
LEQ (%)	57,512	−503,500	650,100	−1,051	7,729	−691	−200	−37
CCF (%)	57,512	0	9,471	133	89	108	123	144
EADF (%)	57,512	0	66,300	176	408	127	150	188

Table 2. Summary Statistics of Open Accounts with Different Undrawn Amounts

Undrawn Amount	=$0 (N=11,056)		≤$50 (N=15,945)		>$50 (N=66,026)	
Variable	Mean	Median	Mean	Median	Mean	Median
Account Information at Default						
LEQ (%)	-	-	4,262	1,888	242	151
CCF (%)	196	136	178	159	373	134
EADF (%)	196	136	175	153	110	110
EAD ($)	2,172	1,138	1,754	966	4,044	2,025
Util (%)	118	100	134	120	113	100
Borrower Attributes 12 Months Prior to Default						
Score0	517	515	549	546	610	603
AggCardBal0 ($)	5,355	2,134	6,444	2,371	13,441	5,919
AggCardUtil0 (%)	91	100	87	94	66	75
AggHEBal0 ($)	3,787	0	3,343	0	6,581	0
Inq0	2	1	2	1	2	1
NumAcnt0	1	1	2	1	2	1
Account Information 12 Months Prior to Default						
Util0 (%)	100	100	95	97	67	77
Util0_0	0	0	0.00	0	0.05	0
Util0_95	1	1	0.66	1	0.14	0
Age0 (yrs)	6	6	7	7	8	8
Cred_Amt0 ($)	1,744	824	1,342	561	4,659	2,697
Bal_Amt0 ($)	1,744	824	1,318	536	3,159	1,445
Undrn_Amt0 ($)	0	0	24	23	1,500	362
Pastdue_Amt0 ($)	127	52	18	0	41	0
Payment_Amt0 ($)	55	27	42	21	86	44
High_Bal0 ($)	1,759	827	1,432	601	4,095	2,277
Chgoff_Amt0 ($)	2	0	1	0	4	0

Table 3. Summary Statistics of Open Accounts with Undrawn Amounts > $50

Variable	Current (N=54,955)				Delinquent (N=11,071)			
	Mean	25th Pctl	Median	75th Pctl	Mean	25th Pctl	Median	75th Pctl
Account Information at Default								
LEQ	262	45	170	405	142	7	61	221
CCF	421	118	138	202	148	106	118	143
EADF	114	83	114	137	89	63	93	113
EAD	4,161	794	2,090	5,850	3,466	731	1,764	4,768
Util	118	90	102	123	85	65	94	100
Borrower Attributes 12 Months prior to Default								
Score0	619	561	613	670	563	519	558	603
AggCardBal0	14,770	1,768	6,948	19,144	6,842	572	2,626	7,966
AggCardUtil0	67	50	75	90	63	33	74	93
AggHEBal0	6,882	0	0	0	5,082	0	0	0
Inq0	2	0	1	2	2	0	1	2
NumAcnt0	2	0	2	3	2	0	1	3
Account Information 12 Months prior to Default								
Util0	66	49	77	91	69	54	78	90
Util0_0	0.06	0	0	0	0.01	0	0	0
Util0_95	0.14	0	0	0	0.12	0	0	0
Age0	8	5	7	10	9.18	6	8	12
Dlq0	0	0	0	0	2.27	1	2	3
Cred_Amt0	4,674	773	2,660	6,700	4,586	915	2,705	6,500
Bal_Amt0	3,168	371	1,431	4,563	3,114	498	1,537	4,427
Undrn_Amt0	1,506	142	356	1,359	1,472	152	394	1,415
Pastdue_Amt0	2	0	0	0	238	30	95	300
Payment_Amt0	84	15	42	112	97	20	54	125
High_Bal0	4,079	666	2,227	5,846	4,180	851	2,500	5,845
Chgoff_Amt0	4	0	0	0	2	0	0	0

Table 4. Changes in Credit Limit and Balance as Borrowers Approach Default

Months prior to Default	12	9	6	3
# Observations	152,657	38,522	27,375	20,136
Credit Limit Cutback Probability	7.9%	6.9%	6.3%	5.1%
Credit Limit Increase Probability	29.6%	37.5%	14.9%	13.2%
Balance Increase Probability	88.4%	81.2%	72.6%	65.3%
% Change in Credit Limit				
Mean	24.9%	28.9%	7.8%	4.2%
Median	0.0%	0.0%	0.0%	0.0%
% Change in Balances				
Mean	144.2%	105.3%	33.5%	3.3%
Median	31.0%	30.0%	13.9%	4.7%
LEQ				
Mean	166.3%	−160.5%	1.5%	−72.6%
Median	21.0%	0.0%	0.0%	−6.9%
CCF				
Mean	244.2%	205.3%	133.5%	103.3%
Median	131.0%	130.0%	113.9%	104.7%
EADF				
Mean	147.5%	138.4%	113.1%	100.4%
Median	130.5%	129.2%	111.0%	104.9%

Table 5. Changes in Credit Limit and Balance for Open Accounts with Different Undrawn Amounts and Delinquency Status

Open Accounts

Undrawn Amount	=0 (N=11,056)		≤$50 (N=15,945)		>$50 (N=66,026)	
Variable	Mean	Median	Mean	Median	Mean	Median
Credit Limit Cutback Probability	16.5%	-	5.6%	-	12.4%	-
Credit Limit Increase Probability	79.2%	-	41.0%	-	26.1%	-
% Change in Credit Limit	86.0%	29.0%	44.0%	0.0%	11.5%	0.0%
Balance Increase Probability	93.4%	-	92.1%	-	88.5%	-
% Change in Balances	96.2%	36.0%	78.1%	58.7%	273.4%	34.2%

Open Accounts with Undrawn Amounts > $50

	Current (N=54,955)		Delinquent (N=11,071)	
Variable	Mean	Median	Mean	Median
Credit Limit Cutback Probability	13.5%	-	6.9%	-
Credit Limit Increase Probability	26.9%	-	22.3%	-
% Change in Credit Limit	12.8%	0.0%	5.2%	0.0%
Balance Increase Probability	89.0%	-	85.7%	-
% Change in Balances	321.2%	38.3%	47.7%	18.0%

Delinquent Open Accounts with Undrawn Amounts > $50

	1 month (N=4,219)		2 month (N=2,782)		3 month (N=1,845)	
Variable	Mean	Median	Mean	Median	Mean	Median
Credit Limit Cutback Probability	10.7%	-	7.7%	-	2.8%	-
Credit Limit Increase Probability	29.8%	-	21.1%	-	17.7%	-
% Change in Credit Limit	8.0%	0.0%	4.4%	0.0%	2.8%	0.0%
Balance Increase Probability	89.0%	-	87.0%	-	83.8%	-
% Change in Balances	65.9%	27.1%	57.3%	19.1%	24.0%	13.7%

	4 month (N=1,258)		5 month (N=967)	
Variable	Mean	Median	Mean	Median
Credit Limit Cutback Probability	2.1%	-	1.8%	-
Credit Limit Increase Probability	13.5%	-	13.2%	-
% Change in Credit Limit	1.9%	0.0%	3.6%	0.0%
Balance Increase Probability	80.5%	-	78.5%	-
% Change in Balances	23.7%	8.6%	17.2%	4.2%

Table 6. Correlations for Current and Open Accounts with Undrawn Amounts > $50

	LEQ	EAD	Score0	AggCardUtil0	Inq0	NumAcnt0	AggCardBal0	AggHEBal0	Util0	Util0_0	Util0_95	Age0	Cred_Amt0	Bal_Amt0	Pastdue_Amt0	Payment_Amt0	High_Bal0	Chgoff_Amt0	QRE_DftRate0	Rush_to_File
EAD	**0.190**	1																		
Score0	**-0.108**	**0.278**	1																	
AggCardUtil0	**0.125**	0.033	**-0.442**	1																
Inq0	0.031	0.000	**-0.168**	0.036	1															
NumAcnt0	-0.032	**0.099**	**0.122**	0.001	0.052	1														
AggCardBal0	-0.003	**0.470**	**0.126**	**0.181**	0.043	**0.235**	1													
AggHEBal0	_-0.008_	**0.139**	**0.087**	_0.008_	**0.097**	0.039	**0.203**	1												
Util0	**0.173**	**0.255**	**-0.238**	**0.491**	-0.021	0.015	**0.165**	0.017	1											
Util0_0	**-0.037**	**-0.080**	**0.153**	**-0.239**	0.043	0.010	-0.042	0.009	**-0.528**	1										
Util0_95	**0.212**	**0.295**	-0.011	**0.193**	0.003	0.062	**0.205**	0.040	**0.410**	-0.097	1									
Age0	-0.060	**0.193**	**0.161**	**-0.049**	**-0.123**	**0.114**	**0.181**	_-0.007_	-0.006	-0.025	0.051	1								
Cred_Amt0	**-0.051**	**0.809**	**0.449**	**-0.133**	-0.047	**0.123**	**0.456**	**0.137**	0.046	-0.039	**0.192**	**0.299**	1							
Bal_Amt0	0.024	**0.874**	**0.255**	0.091	-0.031	**0.109**	**0.501**	**0.139**	**0.404**	**-0.180**	**0.369**	**0.234**	**0.840**	1						
Pastdue_Amt0	-0.012	0.027	-0.033	-0.006	0.002	-0.003	-0.006	-0.002	**0.020**	-0.014	0.015	0.018	0.031	0.036	1					
Payment_Amt0	0.042	**0.765**	**0.199**	0.096	-0.035	0.086	**0.425**	**0.136**	**0.364**	**-0.169**	**0.325**	**0.193**	**0.729**	**0.866**	0.040	1				
High_Bal0	-0.014	**0.842**	**0.332**	-0.010	-0.028	**0.118**	**0.490**	**0.156**	**0.227**	**-0.108**	**0.281**	**0.280**	**0.902**	**0.913**	0.037	**0.803**	1			
Chgoff_Amt0	-0.019	-0.001	-0.013	0.004	0.000	-0.011	-0.009	-0.005	0.011	-0.003	0.006	0.039	0.007	0.011	0.042	0.005	-0.002	1		
QRE_DftRate0	**0.020**	**-0.049**	**-0.072**	0.037	-0.023	0.013	-0.044	-0.079	0.001	-0.008	-0.011	**0.109**	**-0.063**	**-0.055**	-0.006	**-0.101**	**-0.072**	0.002	1	
Rush_to_File	0.006	**-0.034**	-0.028	0.035	-0.037	_-0.007_	-0.029	-0.027	0.021	-0.025	_-0.007_	-0.014	**-0.044**	-0.030	0.009	-0.044	-0.043	_-0.008_	**-0.256**	1
Post_BAPCP	_-0.008_	**0.141**	**0.172**	**-0.111**	0.012	-0.012	**0.094**	**0.103**	-0.024	0.014	0.016	**-0.229**	**0.175**	**0.138**	0.001	**0.174**	**0.187**	-0.019	**-0.322**	**-0.356**

Boldface numbers are significant at 5 percent level and underlined numbers are significant at 10 percent level.

35

Table 7. Correlations for Delinquent and Open Accounts with Undrawn Amounts > $50

	LEQ	EAD	Score0	AggCard Util0	Inq0	Num Acnt0	AggCard Bal0	AggHE Bal0	Util0	Util0_0	Util0_95	Dlq0	Age0	Cred_ Amt0	Bal_ Amt0	Pastdue _Amt0	Payment _Amt0	High _Bal0	Chgoff _Amt0	QRE_ DftRate0	Rush_ to_File
EAD	0.168	1																			
Score0	-0.088	0.229	1																		
AggCardUtil0	0.107	0.001	-0.409	1																	
Inq0	0.012	0.056	-0.159	0.056	1																
NumAcnt0	-0.020	0.133	0.234	-0.003	0.104	1															
AggCardBal0	0.027	0.403	0.057	0.249	0.089	0.234	1														
AggHEBal0	-0.007	0.099	0.073	0.016	0.045	0.062	0.187	1													
Util0	0.165	0.354	-0.216	0.344	0.040	0.001	0.158	0.016	1												
Util0_0	-0.004	-0.020	0.001	-0.028	-0.004	-0.012	-0.019	-0.009	-0.201	1											
Util0_95	0.166	0.345	0.023	0.082	0.038	0.051	0.180	0.050	0.397	-0.030	1										
Dlq0	-0.069	0.063	-0.028	-0.135	-0.086	-0.022	-0.096	-0.020	-0.051	0.013	0.003	1									
Age0	-0.089	0.156	0.194	-0.109	-0.027	0.098	0.061	-0.010	-0.100	0.032	0.015	0.104	1								
Cred_Amt0	-0.057	0.804	0.387	-0.164	0.031	0.153	0.347	0.104	-0.022	-0.024	0.186	0.128	0.256	1							
Bal_Amt0	0.006	0.958	0.246	-0.005	0.056	0.137	0.407	0.103	0.375	-0.062	0.362	0.081	0.176	0.836	1						
Pastdue_Amt0	-0.008	0.709	0.168	-0.054	0.077	0.083	0.227	0.073	0.230	-0.047	0.225	0.308	0.110	0.658	0.743	1					
Payment_Amt0	0.020	0.765	0.205	0.005	0.032	0.108	0.354	0.083	0.288	-0.019	0.293	0.067	0.147	0.665	0.790	0.616	1				
High_Bal0	-0.036	0.859	0.317	-0.083	0.051	0.144	0.389	0.112	0.159	-0.022	0.268	0.097	0.237	0.889	0.898	0.688	0.711	1			
Chgoff_Amt0	0.002	0.014	0.026	-0.028	-0.002	0.010	-0.010	-0.004	-0.018	-0.002	0.014	0.004	0.040	0.007	0.001	-0.003	-0.004	0.012	1		
QRE_DftRate0	0.048	-0.090	-0.127	0.064	0.008	-0.012	-0.082	-0.064	0.027	0.005	-0.034	-0.007	0.061	-0.123	-0.105	-0.107	-0.136	-0.127	0.022	1	
Rush_to_File	0.010	-0.062	-0.074	0.056	0.002	-0.018	-0.062	-0.027	0.017	-0.013	-0.016	0.008	-0.034	-0.083	-0.066	-0.039	-0.105	-0.088	-0.006	-0.250	1
Post_BAPCP	-0.032	0.203	0.235	-0.135	-0.001	0.029	0.118	0.087	-0.045	-0.055	0.047	0.030	-0.151	0.269	0.214	0.240	0.187	0.264	-0.019	-0.316	-0.416

Boldface numbers are significant at 5 percent level and underlined numbers are significant at 10 percent level.

Table 8. Regression: Current and Open Accounts with Undrawn Amounts > $50

Dependent Variable: LEQ

Variable	All Variables		Stepwise	
	All Observations (Model 1)	Outliers Excluded (Model 2)	All Observations (Model 3)	Outliers Excluded (Model 4)
Intercept	**197.038**	**160.151**	**192.547**	**152.421**
Score0	**−0.439**	**−0.284**	**−0.417**	**−0.250**
AggCardBal0	**−0.001**	**−0.001**	**−0.001**	**−0.001**
AggCardUtil0	**0.464**	**0.707**	**0.453**	**0.693**
AggHEBal0	0.000	0.000		
Inq0	3.576	**3.018**	3.427	**2.939**
NumAcnt0	**−7.846**	**−6.990**	**−7.813**	**−6.989**
Util0	**3.459**	**3.652**	**3.338**	**3.453**
Util0_0	**197.994**	**140.533**	**194.568**	**135.520**
Util0_95	**396.156**	**600.594**	**394.748**	**598.859**
Age0	**−7.747**	**−8.225**	**−7.657**	**−7.997**
Cred_Amt0	**0.005**	**0.006**		
Bal_Amt0	**−0.028**	**−0.018**	**−0.028**	**−0.016**
Pastdue_Amt0	**−0.268**	**−0.307**	**−0.269**	**−0.306**
Payment_Amt0	**0.749**	0.031	**0.748**	0.032
High_Bal0	**−0.005**	**−0.004**		
Chgoff_Amt0	**−0.089**	**−0.053**	**−0.087**	**−0.051**
QRE_DftRate0	**118.257**	**55.779**	**118.971**	**57.413**
Rush_to_File	**57.061**	2.291	**57.292**	3.120
Post_BAPCP	**−40.802**	**−20.880**	**−40.846**	**−20.769**
F-value	**135.05**	**1119.3**	**160.05**	**1324.66**
Adj. R-sq	0.0648	0.3697	0.0648	0.3690
N	36,753	36,219	36,753	36,220

Boldface numbers are significant at 5 percent level and underlined numbers are significant at 10 percent level.

Table 9. Regression: Delinquent and Open Accounts with Undrawn Amounts > $50

Dependent Variable: LEQ

Variable	All Variables		Stepwise	
	All Observations (Model 1)	Outliers Excluded (Model 2)	All Observations (Model 3)	Outliers Excluded (Model 4)
Intercept	−83.595	−67.887	**−106.287**	**−76.960**
Score0	−0.036	−0.034		
AggCardBal0	−0.001	0.001		
AggCardUtil0	0.292	**0.304**		
AggHEBal0	−0.001	−0.0003	−0.001	−0.0003
Inq0	−2.105	−0.874		
NumAcnt0	−2.627	**−3.395**		
Util0	**2.839**	**3.078**	**2.981**	**3.278**
Util0_0	**189.594**	**161.488**	**198.695**	**162.114**
Util0_95	**234.301**	**338.788**	**231.511**	**337.918**
Dlq0_2	**−32.343**	**−34.835**	**−30.455**	**−37.440**
Dlq0_3	**−71.386**	**−72.008**	**−67.896**	**−77.374**
Dlq0_4	**−80.868**	**−94.675**	**−76.247**	**−102.409**
Dlq0_5	**−76.039**	**−92.905**	**−69.528**	**−102.515**
Age0	**−7.585**	**−5.078**	**−7.871**	**−5.535**
Cred_Amt0	0.005	**0.009**	0.006	**0.007**
Bal_Amt0	**−0.021**	**−0.017**	**−0.019**	**−0.023**
Pastdue_Amt0	0.031	**−0.030**		
Payment_Amt0	−0.013	**−0.071**		
High_Bal0	0.0026	−0.003		
Chgoff_Amt0	0.018	0.014		
QRE_DftRate0	**144.933**	**101.959**	**150.894**	**101.475**
Rush_to_File	**60.989**	**22.403**	**66.293**	**21.162**
Post_BAPCP	**−73.383**	**−53.223**	**−74.665**	**−56.995**
F-value	**24.91**	**131.05**	**40.34**	**211.4**
Adj. R-sq	0.0727	0.3003	0.0728	0.2971
N	7,019	6,971	7,019	6,971

Boldface numbers are significant at 5 percent level and **underlined numbers** are significant at 10 percent level.

Table 10. Comparison of Predictive Accuracy of Alternative LEQ Models and Methods

		Current		Delinquent	
		RMSE (in sample)	**RMSE (out of sample)**	**RMSE (in sample)**	**RMSE (out of sample)**
	N	**36,753**	**18,202**	**7,019**	**4,052**
Model 1	All variables (all obs)	765.33	720.27	472.00	640.21
Model 2	All variables (no outliers)	769.76	713.23	474.46	630.63
Model 3	Stepwise (all obs)	765.35	720.19	472.28	641.54
Model 4	Stepwise (no outliers)	769.83	713.25	474.26	630.59
Common Industry Practices					
Model 5	Regression (censored)	810.20	766.24	493.68	641.86
Average	Censored	813.49	769.08	499.53	643.48
Average	Raw	791.39	746.86	490.95	639.83

In sample: file years 1999–2006, which contain defaults that occurred from July 1, 1998, to June 30, 2006. Out of sample: file years 2007 and 2008, which contain defaults that occurred from July 1, 2006, to June 30, 2008.

Appendix. Variable Definitions

Name	Description
LEQ	Loan Equivalent, the difference between balance at default and the balance 12 months prior to default as a percentage of undrawn balance 12 months prior to default (%)
CCF	Credit Conversion Factor, balance at default as a percentage of balance 12 months prior to default (%)
EADF	EAD Factor, balance at default as a percentage of credit limit 12 months prior to default (%)
Score0	Generic bureau-based credit score, ranging from 300 to 900, observed 12 months prior to default; higher score means lower risk
AggCardBal0	Aggregate balance for open bankcard tradelines 12 months prior to default ($)
AggCardUtil0	Aggregate balance to credit limit ratio for open bankcard tradelines, 12 months prior to default ($)
AggHEBal0	Aggregate balance for open home equity tradelines 12 months prior to default ($)
Inq0	Number of inquiries within 6 months, observed 12 months prior to default
NumAcnt0	Total number of open retail tradelines within 12 months, observed 12 months prior to default
EAD	Exposure at Default, the larger of credit balance at default and chargeoff amount at default ($)
Util	Credit limit utilization rate of the account at default (%)
Close0	Dummy variable for accounts that were closed 12 months prior to default
Overlimit0	Dummy variable for accounts that have balance amount greater than credit limit 12 months prior to default
Util0	Account credit limit utilization rate (Bal_Amt0/Cred_Amt0) 12 months prior to default (%)
Util0_0	Dummy variable for accounts with 0% utilization rate 12 months prior to default
Util0_95	Dummy variable for accounts with utilization rate >95% 12 months prior to default
Age0	Number of years since account opened 12 months prior to default
Cred_Amt0	Credit limit of the account 12 months prior to default
Bal_Amt0	Credit balance of the account, including late charges and fees, 12 months prior to default ($)
Undrn_Amt0	The difference between credit limit (Cred_Amt0) and credit balance (Bal_Amt0)
Pastdue_Amt0	Amount past due of the account, including late charges and fees, excluding current amount, 12 months prior to default ($)
Payment_Amt0	Monthly payment amount on the account 12 months prior to default ($)
High_Bal0	Highest balance ever attained on the account up to 12 months prior to default ($)
Chgoff_Amt0	Amount charged off on the account 12 months prior to default ($)
QRE_DftRate	Quarterly default rate of all qualifying revolving exposures (QREs) in the database (%)
Rush_to_File	Dummy for the period with elevated aggregate QRE default rate from April 20, 2005, when the Bankruptcy Abuse Prevention and Consumer Protection Act was signed into law, to October 17, 2005, when the law was implemented
Post_BAPCP	Dummy for the period after the Bankruptcy Abuse Prevention and Consumer Protection Act of 2005 became effective on October 17, 2005